MW01268638

YOU CAN LIVE ABOVE
YOUR CIRCUMSTANCES

YOU
CAN LIVE
ABOVE
Your Circumstances

HERMAN W. GOCKEL

Publishing House
St. Louis London

Unless otherwise indicated, New Testament quotations are from *Good News for Modern Man: The New Testament in Today's English Version,* published by the American Bible Society. Quotations from the King James Version are marked KJV. A few quotations from *The New Testament in Modern English,* by J. B. Phillips, are marked "Phillips."

Concordia Publishing House, St. Louis, Missouri
Concordia Publishing House Ltd., London, E. C. 1
Copyright © 1973 Concordia Publishing House
Library of Congress Catalog No. 72-96741
ISBN 0-570-03154-0

MANUFACTURED IN THE UNITED STATES OF AMERICA

PREFACE

Herman W. Gockel has done it again! He certainly is able to tell the good news of Jesus Christ with clarity and style. When Dr. Gockel says it, anybody can get it.

This new book by the man who was program director of television's "This Is the Life" for its first twenty years (1951 – 1971) is sprightly in style, serving not only to inform but also to entertain the reader. It is a great art to tell the Gospel in such a way as to make pleasant reading. It is the art of the New Testament itself, which has a fascination all its own.

Seldom does one find such a highly developed popular style and such deep theological insights combined in one writer. Dr. Gockel knows Jesus Christ, and he doesn't mind telling people about Him. In fact he enjoys doing that!

Jesus Christ makes it possible for people to live "above" their circumstances, rather than to endure life "under" those circumstances. Jesus Christ makes a man a real man, and a woman a real woman.

Dr. Gockel has found it out for himself and it is in this book: you don't have to run away from yourself, you can find something to live for, you can get rhyme and reason out of your life, you can be good for something, you have got something to celebrate, and you had better believe it.

This book comes from the Bible. It is about Jesus Christ. It is evangelical, grounded in the Word of God. It is human, easy to read, and — with no loss of reverence for the holy — entertaining. It is Herman W. Gockel at his ever living best.

December 19, 1972

OSWALD C. J. HOFFMANN

CONTENTS

CHAPTER ONE

You Can Live
Above Your Circumstances

So you're doing all right—"under the circumstances"!

That's fine. But did you know there are people in this world who do not *have* to live under their circumstances, but can live *above* them?

They're in the minority, it's true. Most of us are still living *under* our circumstances. Our spirits are up when the doctor bill is paid, down when it's unpaid. All the world looks bright and sunny when our digestion's good; all is dark and gloomy the minute there's the slightest disagreement between our touchy stomach and the last unfriendly morsel we have fed it.

For many of us life is a series of ups and downs, and our spirits seem to chart a course which is exactly parallel. An unexpected bonus—and our spirits zoom to the stratosphere! A shocking telegram—and immediately they go into a tailspin! A new job—and the future is bright with promise! A week in bed with the flu—and we begin to wonder if life is worth living after all!

Like a Jack-in-the-box, many of us are living under the ceiling of our circumstances. Up when the pressure is off. Down when the pressure is on.

God has given us a way of living *above* that ceiling. That way is to be found in the Christian Gospel. If there was ever a man who had learned to live above his circumstances, that man was the apostle Paul, the man who had met the resurrected and ascended Christ on the road to Damascus and who spent every day of the rest of his life telling others about his great discovery — the man, by the way, who was later inspired to write thirteen of the sixty-six books that make up our Bible.

It would be difficult to imagine a life that had more *downs* than Paul's. At least, it is improbable that anyone who reads these pages has had to experience the succession of hard knocks that seemed to lie in wait for Paul at almost every turn. Toward the end of his life he wrote a letter to a group of people in Corinth, a city in Greece, and near the close of that letter he took time out to list some of the hardships he had had to endure. Listen as he counts them out one by one:

"I have been in prison more times [than his detractors]," he says. "I have been whipped much more, and I have been near death more often. Five times I was given the thirty-nine lashes by the Jews; three times I was whipped by the Romans, and once I was stoned; I have been in three shipwrecks, and once I spent twenty-four hours in the water.

"In my many travels I have been in danger from floods and from robbers, in danger from fellow Jews and from Gentiles; there have been dangers in the cities, dangers in the wilds, dangers on the high seas, and dangers from false friends. There has been work and toil; often I have gone without sleep; I have been hungry and thirsty; I have often been without enough food, shelter, or clothing." (2 Cor. 11:23-27)

Paul would have been a dejected and disheartened man, indeed, if he had had to live *under* those circumstances. If he was going to live happily and victoriously, he would have to live above them. He would have to find a vantage point from which he could view the entire panorama of his life in its relation to the divine pattern, of which we shall speak in detail in a later chapter. Above all, he would have to find a source of spiritual power which would give him the strength and fortitude not only to cope with these difficult circumstances but also, and especially, to conquer and overcome them. Fortunately for Paul, he found that power. He found it in the Gospel of Jesus Christ.

After years of experience in the Christian way of life, he wrote to some of his friends: "I have learned to be satisfied with what I have. I know what it is to be in need, and what it is to have more than enough. I have learned this secret, so that anywhere, at any time, I am content, whether I am full or hungry, whether I have too much or too little. I have the strength to face *all* conditions by the power that Christ gives me." (Phil. 4:11-13)

It was Christ who gave Paul the power to face and to overcome "all conditions" of life. The Christ *for* him and the Christ *in* him. As he wrote on another occasion: "It is no longer I who live, but it is Christ who lives in me. This life that I live now, I live by faith in the Son of God, who loved me and gave His life for me." (Gal. 2:20)

That was Paul's secret. He had been overcome

by the love of God as revealed through Jesus Christ, and in that surrender all of the circumstances of his life, too, had been overcome. Once he had been convinced that God actually loved him and that, through Christ, God had accepted him as one of His children, Paul was prepared to face all of life's perplexities. From that moment on he knew that there was only one circumstance in life that he would have to live *under* — and that was the circumstance of God's love.

In the death of Christ on the cross, a death in which Paul saw God's own payment for everything that he, Paul, had done wrong, he saw proof positive that God's attitude toward him was one of fatherly affection and tender mercy. And that was all he needed to know. To know that God really loved him, that God's own Son had lived and died and risen again *for him* and had insured for him a future of eternal bliss and happiness, that was enough! The revelation of the Christian Gospel had convinced Paul, once and for all times, that God was *for* him, that God was on his side.

That was the fundamental circumstance under which his entire life was lived — after his conversion on the Damascus road. And from that overwhelming circumstance he reasoned with justifiable logic: "If God is for us, who can be against us? He did not even keep back His own Son, but offered Him for us all! . . . will He not also freely give us all things?" (Rom. 8:31-32)

In other words, if God has given us the GIFT, will He not also let us have the ribbons? If He has given us His Son to die for us, to win us back to fellowship with Him, and to prepare for us a place in the Father's house above, surely He'll find a way to help us pay our doctor bills, to feed and clothe our children, and to keep a sheltering roof above our head. If He has done the greater thing, surely we can count on Him to do the lesser. And even if, for reasons known only to Him, we should be called upon to suffer poverty, sickness, and dire calamity, we know that among the "all things" He has promised are the needed patience, strength, and fortitude to emerge victorious over even these most difficult circumstances.

That, to put it simply, was the great and overpowering secret of Paul's life. He had been thoroughly convinced of the love of God as revealed by the life and death and resurrection of His Son. With that conviction firmly rooted in his heart, he could conquer every circumstance of life. Listen to the bold and confident assurance of this first-century hero of the faith who had learned to live above his circumstances:

"Who, then, can separate us from the love of Christ?" he challenges. "Can trouble do it, or hardship, or persecution, or hunger, or poverty, or danger, or death? . . . No, in all these things we have complete victory through Him who loved us! For I am certain that nothing can separate us from His love: neither death nor life; neither angels nor other heavenly rulers or powers; neither the present nor the future; neither the world above nor the world below — there is nothing in all creation that will ever be able to separate us from the love of God which is ours through Christ Jesus our Lord." (Rom. 8:35-39)

Amid life's most trying circumstances the believer in Christ is assured of complete and final victory. What confidence! What assurance! "Conquerors —through Him that loved us." What a victory! What a life! This is the kind of life that awaits every man, woman, or child who will put his faith in the Christian Gospel: a life which surmounts the vexations and frustrations of daily living and is assured of ultimate victory through the power of Christ—who loves us.

The man who is living under *that* circumstance can live above all others.

CHAPTER TWO

You Can Tap the Real Source of Spiritual Power

Have you ever walked down a city street which was lined with giant sycamores? Rising high on either side, like pillars in a huge cathedral, they extend their leafy arms across the street — until they form a canopy of green, affording shade throughout the summer months.

We spent most of our childhood and youth on a street like that. We can well remember how, at regular intervals, there stood a shabby telephone pole — splintered, gashed, and weather-beaten. Although it stood as erect as the sycamores, it sprouted no branches, produced no leaves, and contributed nothing to the gorgeous symphony of green and brown and yellow which thrilled the heart of every passerby.

Why the difference? The answer, of course, is simple. The sycamores had roots, and the telephone poles had none. The sycamores had tapped an unseen source below the ground from which they drew their daily nourishment, while the telephone pole was merely a piece of lifeless wood sunk into the earth.

In a sense more real than may at first be apparent, the man who has put his faith in Christ is just like one of those sycamores. He has sunk his roots deep into

15

the promises of God, and in those promises he has found the power which has transformed his life into a fresh and growing vital thing. In the familiar words of the Bible, he is "like a tree planted by the rivers of water, that bringeth forth his fruit in his season; his leaf also shall not wither, and whatsoever he doeth shall prosper." (Ps. 1:3 **KJV**)

You, too, can tap the only source of regenerating and vitalizing spiritual power. That source is Christ! The Savior was doing more than painting a pretty word picture when He said: "I am the vine, you are the branches. Whoever remains in Me, and I in him, will bear much fruit; for you can do nothing without Me." (John 15:5)

Fortunately for the world, and for all of us, the Man who made that statement had the necessary credentials to back it up. Christ was no mere man, no mere superstar, no mere greatest among the great. Of Him the Bible says: "He was shown with great power *to be the Son of God,* by being raised from death" (Rom. 1:4). As the Son of God with great power, Christ has, indeed, proved Himself to be the Vine from which millions upon millions of believers down through the ages have drawn their spiritual strength.

Among the first to experience the transforming and vitalizing power of Christ were the faithful few who had believed in Him during the three short years of His earthly ministry. If ever there was a band of defeated, dejected, and frightened men, it was the hopeless, hapless little group of eleven disciples whose world had collapsed when their Master died. Like frightened sheep, they were huddled in a back room on a side street in the city of Jerusalem — weak, timid, quaking, afraid of their own shadows!

But what a difference when once they had been assured that Christ had arisen from the dead! All of a sudden the future which to them had seemed so empty and lonely had been transformed into a radiant present, charged with the power of His sustaining presence. No matter where they went from that time on, they knew that the omnipresent and omnipotent Christ was with them. No combination of evil powers could successfully withstand them. They had become conscious of a tremendous inner power hitherto unknown to them; the power of the conquering Christ.

And so they went forth to live courageous and victorious lives. Peter, the weakling who had deserted his Lord in the moment of His greatest need, all of a sudden becomes a fearless preacher of the Gospel. Stephen stands like a pillar and is unafraid. John preaches boldly in the Temple. And Saul of Tarsus sets out to turn the world upside down for Christ. "You will receive power," Christ had told them. Now they had received that power.

And so can you!

How? By building your life firmly and squarely on the eternal promises of God, as these have been certified by Jesus Christ. Christ is the Guarantor of every gracious promise in the Scriptures! In a sense, the Bible is the offer of a spiritual bank account on which the believer in Christ is free to draw at any time. Most important of the spiritual assets which have been written to the believer's credit in the bank of heaven is the endless supply of divine forgiveness which has been earned for him by his divine Redeemer (Rom.

4:3-8, 20-25). The Bible tells him: "Though your sins be as scarlet, they shall be as white as snow; though they be red like crimson, they shall be as wool" (Is. 1:18 KJV). And why? Because "the blood of Jesus, His Son, makes us clean from every sin" (1 John 1:7). That is the primary, the fundamental, promise of the Scriptures: the offer of full and free forgiveness of every wrong we've ever done, the complete removal of every stain of guilt, through faith in Jesus Christ, the Savior. You are at liberty to draw on that promise whenever you like, no matter what you've done, no matter what your "circumstance" in life may be.

And there are countless other gilt-edged promises (from God to you) in the Bible. "I will never leave thee nor forsake thee" (Heb. 13:5 KJV). "Remember! I will be with you always" (Matt. 28:20). "My presence shall go with thee" (Ex. 33:14 KJV). "Fear thou not, for I am with thee; be not dismayed, for I am thy God. I will strengthen thee; yea, I will help thee; yea, I will uphold thee with the right hand of My righteousness" (Is. 41:10 KJV). "Call upon Me in the day of trouble; I will deliver thee" (Ps. 50:15 KJV). "There shall no evil befall thee, neither shall any plague come nigh thy dwelling." (Ps. 91:10 KJV)

"Empty promises," did you say? By no means! Christ Himself has placed the seal of heaven upon them! Since Christ has affixed His signature to every promise of the Father, you can rest assured that they *are* the Father's promises and that they will be kept. The apostle Paul put it this way: "Jesus Christ . . . is the divine 'Yes.' Every promise of God finds its affirmative in Him." (2 Cor. 1:19-20 Phillips)

This is one of the distinctive dimensions of the Christian faith. Its assurances are not of the greeting card variety, but they have the signature of the Son of God Himself. He who lived and died and rose again has said: "Yes, these promises are true. My Father will fulfill them."

To keep the channel clear for the inflowing power of God, you must keep the channel clear between yourself and Christ. He is the Vine. Through Him, and through Him alone, we live in daily contact with the Eternal. Through Him, and only through Him, we can dip our empty lives into God's fullness and come up with that power which we need to see the daily struggle through.

In his beautiful hymn "Jesus, Lover of My Soul," Charles Wesley has two significant lines which have become the earnest prayer of every believer in Christ:

> Reach me out Thy gracious hand,
> While I of Thy strength receive.

We are reminded, every time we repeat those lines, of a novel diversion which became popular shortly after the invention of the electric battery. It was considered an innocent form of entertainment to have one member of the family hold the positive wire of a series of batteries while another took hold of the negative wire. To close the circuit, other members of the family were invited to join hands and to complete the circle. As soon as the last hand was clasped, there was a sudden tingling surge — the symptom of a current of electrical power coursing through the body. Imperfect and inadequate though the parallel may be, we have here at least a weak analogy of the profound spiritual truth which Charles Wesley voiced in the lines quoted above.

> Reach me out Thy gracious hand,
> While I of Thy strength receive.

The Christian has put his hand into the strong right hand of Christ. In the language of the popular opera, he has by an act of conscious faith "put his hand in the hand of the Man who stilled the water," and in that hand, the omnipotent hand of the omnipotent Christ, he has found strength: strength to stand upright in a world that is tumbling all around him; strength to walk, erect, into a new day; strength to stand tall despite the pressures of adversity; strength to stand up for what is right; strength to resist temptation in whatever form — or, having fallen, to tread the path of the prodigal back to the Father's house.

One of the last things Christ said to His disciples before He ascended into heaven was: "You will be filled with power" (Acts 1:8). That promise still holds for *you* and for all who remain in contact with Him through faith in His word.

He is still the Vine. We are still the branches. It is still He who enables us to live life to the full, regardless of our circumstances.

We shall close this chapter with what we consider to be a dramatic illustration of the truth we have been trying to bring out in these pages. It happened many years ago. It was a cool October morning in a seaside village in England. A pastor was visiting in a cobbler's shop, watching him pound a piece of leather with a hammer, and listening as the happy cobbler hummed a merry tune.

Looking around the dingy little shop, with its cramped quarters and its crowded shelves, the pastor marveled that the man before him never seemed depressed.

"Man," he finally said, "don't you *ever* get tired of this narrow life—the same thing day after day—in this cramped and crowded little room?"

The cobbler walked to a back door, opened it wide, and said: "Reverend, whenever I start feeling sorry for myself, I just come over here and open this door." As the large, wooden door swung open, the room was flooded with a new glory. Within the twinkling of an eye the cramped little shop had been glorified by the vastness of its new relationship—its oneness with the fields and skies and rolling seas, and with the Creator and Redeemer of them all.

In a sense, it is very much the same with life in general. All of us are in danger of living within the closed doors of our immediate circumstances, looking at the same dark walls day after day, the walls of our own gloomy thoughts, walls which we have placarded with our own "insuperable" problems.

How different, when we *open* the door—and link our little lives to God's eternal purposes, to the whole panorama of His love and grace as revealed in Jesus Christ, our Savior! How different when the fresh air and bright sunlight of God's eternity are permitted to flood into the dark and dingy cubicles of life!

Do our problems look too big for us today? Problems at home? at work? at school? in the office? Are the walls of our life, as it were, closing in on us, crushing out all faith and hope and joy? Open the door!

Look out—look up—look into the vastness of God's love, as He reveals Himself to us in the Gospel of His Son.

The cobbler could open a physical door and immediately establish contact with a world of brightness, joy, and beauty. By God's grace, you and I can open a spiritual door by turning to the precious Gospel of His Son and gaining an entirely new perspective not only for today but for the whole of life. The question is: Have we opened the door?

"Behold, I stand at the door and knock," says Jesus. "If any man hear My voice and open the door, I will come in to him and will sup with him, and he with Me." (Rev. 3:20 KJV)

There, finally, is the real Source of spiritual power.

CHAPTER THREE

You Don't Have
To Run Away from Yourself

Recently a radio company which has manufactured a new, compact little pocket radio ran a full-page newspaper advertisement with the screaming headline: "You need never be alone again!" The man who wrote that heading knew his business. He knew what millions of Americans want—or rather, what they don't want. They want "never to be alone again!"

That is why they spend day after day, night after night, in a frantic effort to run away from themselves. Maybe they don't realize it, or maybe they would be the last ones to admit it, but the fact of the matter is—they can stand almost anybody's company but their own. They just "can't stand" to be by themselves.

And so, like frightened youngsters, they make sure that they are never left alone. By a flick of the switch on their radio or their television set they convert their home into a grand hotel—so that they can live with *other* people's thoughts, *other* people's music, *other* people's conversations. Or they jump into their car, run down to the neighborhood movie, and lose themselves in a land of make-believe by living with the phantom figures on the silver screen.

Anything! Just so they don't have to live with themselves!

Now, what is it about the average person that makes him such unpleasant company for himself? What is it about *you* that makes you so uneasy when all the other noises stop and you begin to listen to yourself? What is it down deep within you that you would like to run away from?

Your conscience? If that's it, we agree: you're not good company—*for you!* Your inner self just isn't fit to live with. No one likes to live in the presence of an electric alarm clock that has gone berserk and refuses to shut off. Nothing could be more nerve-wracking or disconcerting. Did you know that God *has* placed an alarm clock into every human breast in the form of human conscience? When once that clock goes off, there's just no living with it.

One of the great men of the Bible, King David, spent days and weeks in a state of mind which was almost unbearable. He had done something wrong, terribly wrong, and the alarm of his conscience could not be controlled. "When I kept silence," he writes, "my bones waxed old through my roaring all the day long. For day and night Thy hand was heavy upon me. My moisture is turned into the drought of summer" (Ps. 32:3-4 KJV). In another moment of similar depression he wrote: "Oh, that I had wings like a dove, for then would I fly away and be at rest!" (Ps. 55:6 KJV)

David had found that of all the company he could possibly choose, his own guilty conscience was the worst to get along with. It roared at him "all the day long." But he also found that he couldn't run away from it. And neither can you.

Fortunately, you don't *have* to. There are millions

of people in this world who have learned to live with their conscience — not by ignoring it, but by facing up to it and by accepting God's own solution for the endless accusations it presents. What is that solution?

Perhaps the simplest way of showing how a believer in Christ manages to deal with the insistent voice of an accusing conscience is to listen to an imaginary conversation between a believer and that merciless accuser which lurks and leers in every human breast. This, or something similar, is what we would likely hear:

Conscience: You have sinned!

Believer: Where have I sinned?

Conscience: You have broken all of God's commandments. You haven't loved Him with all your heart and soul and mind. You haven't loved your neighbor as yourself. You've dealt unfairly with your parents, unfairly with your children. You've hated, you've cheated, you've slandered, you've been jealous. You've harbored unclean thoughts, spoken unclean words, become guilty of unclean deeds. You've been selfish, greedy, grasping. You've been more concerned with making a good living than making a good life. You've been leaving God out of much of your thinking. You've . . . .

Believer: I agree with every word you say. I'm guilty. I'd be a fool and a liar if I'd try to deny it.

Conscience: And you know what God has· said about people who do such things. "For sin pays its wage — death" (Rom. 6:23). "Whoever does not always obey everything that is written in the book of the Law is under the curse!" (Gal. 3:10). And "the soul that sinneth, it shall die." (Ezek. 18:4 KJV)

25

Believer: Yes, I know. I know that I have sinned, and I know that a righteous God (if He is to remain righteous, and if He is to remain God) must punish every transgression of His righteous will.

Conscience: Therefore you are lost!

Believer: Ah, that's where you are *wrong!* God in His mercy has provided me with a Substitute. This Substitute has assumed my guilt. He has paid my penalty. When He died on the cross, He suffered the pangs of hell for me. And when His Father raised Him from the grave on the third day, He tore up my summons and promised that I shall never be haled into the court of heaven for any misdeed I have done. Because Christ has "made good" for me, I have been declared innocent in the sight of His Father. Begone, conscience, I have work to do!

That simple? Yes, that simple! The Bible puts it this way: "There is therefore now no condemnation to them which are in Christ Jesus" (Rom. 8:1 KJV). "For He hath made Him to be sin for us who knew no sin" (2 Cor. 5:21 KJV). "And the Lord hath laid on Him the iniquity of us all" (Is. 53:6 KJV). "Who would dare to accuse us, whom God has chosen? The Judge Himself has declared us free from sin," (Rom. 8:33 Phillips). Those are the words of Scripture.

Those and a hundred other clear assurances of the Bible are the only means that God has given us to stuff the mouth of a roaring conscience. There *is* no other way of silencing its clamor and making it fit to live with. But does it work?

There are countless people living today who have put their faith in the substitutionary life and death of Jesus Christ and, as a result, have been able to stop running away from the accusations of their conscience. Only God could hold the jaws of the lions when Daniel was thrown into the den. And only God, through the mediation of Christ, can hold the jaws of conscience when conscience leaps at you and me. With Christ — you need not run away.

But Christ not only shuts the mouth of conscience; He fills the heart with pleasant voices. If you have been running away from yourself because you couldn't stand the dull and drab monotony of what you heard within your heart, why not let Christ step inside for just a moment? He'll fill your heart with pleasant company. Instead of the clatter and the clamor of those discordant voices which are driving you nearly to distraction, He'll fill your heart with the gentle voices of "love, joy, peace, patience, kindness, goodness, faithfulness, humility, and self-control." (Gal. 5:22-23)

Have you ever visited in a home where everything was lovely? where every room, every chair, every piece of furniture, gave you that feeling of having been "lived in" and having been enjoyed? where father and mother were living in mutual affection and children were living in respectful obedience to their elders? where all members of the family radiated that warm sense of "belonging" — where all were living for one another? If you did, did the idea of anyone ever wanting to run away from such a home ever occur to you? Most probably not. People just don't *run away* from a home like that.

Neither do people run away from a *life* into which Christ has entered and which He has blessed with the joy, the peace, and the assurance of His presence.

"Behold, I stand at the door and knock," He says; "if any man hear My voice and open the door, I will come in to him and will sup with him, and he with Me." (Rev. 3:20 KJV)

There may still be sorrow in such a life: the sorrow of bereavement, of disappointment, of loneliness, of lingering illness. But the overpowering motif of any life into which Jesus Christ has entered will continue to be the all-pervasive motif of *joy*. Whenever Christ enters a human life, He brings all His trophies with Him: pardon, peace, love, joy, and daily fellowship with Him.

A life which has been blessed with the presence of Christ, let it be repeated, is not the kind of life from which people run away.

CHAPTER FOUR

You Can Find Something to Live For

A young American Air Force captain came back from the war and found it impossible to settle down. Disagreeable at home, dissatisfied at work, and discouraged over his inability to "find himself," he finally went to a psychiatrist.

After a few probing sessions the psychiatrist was rather sure of his diagnosis. "What you lack," he said, "is a *center* around which your life can be integrated." His life had become a lot of spokes without a hub, and until a solid hub could be found there would be no way of regathering the spokes and holding them in place.

A friend directed the young man to a Christian clergyman. Within a very short time he found a center around which he could build his life, for in the quiet of that pastor's study the former Air Force captain, for the first time in his life, was introduced to Christ. And having seen Christ with the eyes of faith, he saw himself in true perspective as he had never seen himself before. Having seen Christ, he soon saw all the loose ends of his life being drawn together around a sure and certain center.

The scattered spokes had found their hub, and one by one they found their place.

Many a life today is pained and twisted—for the lack of a strong and sturdy hub into which to fit its scattered spokes. It has no solid center around which it can group its thoughts, its emotions, its aspirations, and upon which it can build from day to day with purpose and design.

The Gospel of Jesus Christ offers every man a solid center around which, and upon which, to build the structure of his life. The apostle Paul had a great deal to say about this solid "center." At one time he wrote at length to a group of believers in Asia Minor, stressing the importance of keeping all the spokes of their daily living firmly rooted in the hub. "*Christ* is the secret center of our lives," he told them (Col. 3:4 Phillips). And to Paul this "secret center" was more than just a place; it was a power, a passion, and a purpose.

From that center there issued forth a constant flow of power to the perimeter of his everyday activity. From that center there surged a passion for living, for doing, for dying—for Christ. From that center there emanated a constant sense of purpose, an almost Christlike determination to "work the works of Him that sent Me, while it is day," before "the night cometh when no man can work," (John 9:4 KJV)

When Christ takes over at the very center of our life, He gives our life a fundamental, unifying purpose. And when once our life has been given a purpose— God's purpose—it begins to throb with deep and growing satisfactions. The important thing is that we let *Christ* give our life its purpose.

The eminent John Newton once said: "If two angels came down from heaven to execute a divine command, and one was appointed to conduct an empire, while the other was appointed to sweep the streets, they would feel no inclination to change employments." And why not? Because each would have the sure conviction that he was carrying out God's purpose and that by his service, great or small, he was contributing to the achievement of the divine design.

Merely to have a purpose in life is not enough. We must be sure that our purpose is God's purpose. The Bible gives us good examples of two different lives, each centered on an altogether different goal. There was, for instance, the rich man in the parable. He knew very definitely what he was living for. But he was living for the wrong things. His whole life consisted in the abundance of the things he had accumulated—in barns and bales and bank accounts. God placed His own verdict on that kind of life when He said: "You fool!" It will pay you to read this gripping short story in Luke 12:16-21.

An example of the other kind of life we find in the life of the apostle Paul. Those things upon which the rich man had hung his heart meant nothing at all to Paul. And the things which meant nothing to the rich man were the very things that Paul was living for. Paul had hung his heart on something infinitely higher. "For what is life?" he once asked, and then gave this striking reply: "To me, it is Christ!" (Phil. 1:21)

This man Paul had learned the secret of a well-integrated life, a life which was driven by a single motive and focused on a single purpose. For him to live meant only one thing: to live for Christ. The rich man in the parable was all wrapped up in himself. Paul was all wrapped up in Christ. Indeed, Paul once stated that his *real* life and the real life of every true believer is "a hidden one in Christ" (Col. 3:3 Phillips). It seems that Paul couldn't find sufficient prepositions adequately to describe the relationship which existed between Christ and him. He was living *for* Christ, *by* Christ, *in* Christ, *to* Christ. Christ provided him with an all-absorbing purpose for living.

Indeed, Paul knew very definitely what he was living for. And he lived for it with all his might! From a prison cell in Rome he wrote to a group of believers in Philippi, the city where he had been flogged and beaten: "Every advantage that I had gained I considered lost for Christ's sake. Yes, and I look upon *everything* as loss compared with the overwhelming gain of knowing Christ Jesus, my Lord. For His sake I did, in actual fact, suffer the loss of everything, but I considered it useless rubbish compared with being able to win Christ. . . .

"How changed are my ambitions! Now I long to know Christ and the power shown by His resurrection; now I long to share His sufferings, even to die as He died, so that I may perhaps attain, as He did, the resurrection from the dead. Yet, my brothers, I do not consider myself to have 'arrived,' spiritually, nor do I consider myself already perfect. But I keep going on, grasping ever more firmly that purpose for which Christ grasped me." (Phil. 3:7-12 Phillips)

Ever since Christ had overtaken Paul on the Damascus road, Paul had a new reason for living—to "grasp ever more firmly that purpose for which Christ grasped me." Christ had taken hold of Paul's life in order that Paul himself might take hold of the supreme purpose of human existence: to know God and to bring others to that knowledge. Small wonder that this man who had spent his time tracking down the followers of Christ and delivering them to the authorities should now exclaim: "How changed are my ambitions!" His life had been given an entirely different purpose.

Essentially, the purpose of our life is no different from that of the apostle Paul. We are here, first of all, to know God; and, secondly, to serve our fellowman — chiefly by sharing with him the thrill of our great discovery. That is our reason for being. That is what we are here for. That is what we are to live for. That is our *purpose*.

But can a man really know God? Yes, a man can know God if he will listen to the voice of Jesus Christ, His Son. The Bible tells us: "No one has ever seen God at any time. Yet the divine and only Son, who lives in the closest intimacy with the Father, has made Him known" (John 1:18 Phillips). Christ Himself is the revelation of the Father. Christ Himself once said: "Whoever has seen Me has seen the Father" (John 14:9). And on the night before His crucifixion He prayed: "This is eternal life: for men to know You, the only true God, and to know Jesus Christ, whom You sent" (John 17:3). There are millions of people today who have learned to know God as their Father through the revelation of His Son in the pages of the Bible.

And these millions now have one overwhelming purpose for living: by the quality of their lives and by their personal witness to bring others to that knowledge. If you really are looking for something to live for, we suggest that you join hands with those whose consuming passion in life is to live the life of Christ and to spread the good news of salvation through His name. That is something to work for. That is something to *live* for. That will give your life a purpose — its God-intended purpose. And that will give you an inner satisfaction, a sense of purposeful vocation, you have never felt before.

A minister one day was walking by a huge construction project. He asked the first man in overalls what *he* was doing on the project. "I carry bricks" was the curt reply. A moment later he put the same question to another laborer. "I mix the mortar," the second man growled and added a look which said as much as "What business is that of yours?" Just then a younger man walked up, and the minister addressed him with the selfsame question. "And what, my young man, are *you* doing?" With a bright gleam of eager expectation in his eye, the young man looked up to the soaring walls of the rising structure and said: "I'm building a cathedral."

All three men were doing the same thing. And yet they weren't. The younger man had caught a vision which was beyond the grasp of the other two. And having caught the vision, he was no longer merely carrying bricks or mixing mortar; he was building a cathedral. He had caught the glimpse of a glorious *purpose,* and whatever he did from hour to hour was another step toward the achievement of that purpose.

So, too, the life which has been given the vision of God's purposes with men. It is constantly working on a cathedral. Bricks and mortar and sand and gravel there may be. But rising out of them every day are the clear lines of a glorious edifice—a life dedicated to the greater glory of God and to the temporal and eternal welfare of all mankind.

That is something to live for.

That is the life which awaits every man who makes Jesus Christ, the Son of God, "the secret center" of his being.

CHAPTER FIVE

You Can Start Living on Your Surplus

Have you begun to lose your zest for living? Things at the office getting you down? Family problems piling up? World conditions more than you can take? Do you drag yourself to work in the morning as though your first appointment were with an electric chair? Have you lost that spring in your heart, that bounce in your step which John Doe still has and for which you secretly envy him?

If you have, it would be futile, of course, to tell you: "Chin up, shoulders back! Get a spring in your heart and a bounce in your step!" The fact is that until God Himself performs a miracle on your heart and puts a new spring there, your chin isn't going to *stay* up, your shoulders aren't going to *stay* back, and any bounce you might put into your step just isn't going to *stay* there.

Or does that sound too theological?

If so, let me ask: If a man has stomach ulcers and his physician hands him a prescription, would there be any sense in the man's protesting: "That sounds too medical"? Or if a man is in trouble with the income tax department and seeks the guidance of a tax consultant, would there be any point in rejecting the consultant's counsel because it sounds "too legal"?

The fact is that when a man has lost his appetite for living, his problem is basically theological, basically religious, and he had better turn to God for counsel and advice. Only God can create that new life on the *spiritual* level which will give us willingness and joy to carry on on the level of the physical or mental. Until He has created, and unless He sustains, a spiritual life within us, all our efforts at truly "enjoying life" are just so much whistling in the dark.

But God has offered to perform this miracle in human hearts "I have come," says Christ, "in order that they might have life, life in all its fullness" (John 10:10). An equally accurate translation of these remarkable words of the Savior would have been: "I have come that they might have life and that *they might have a surplus of it."*

Anyone who is acquainted with the Christian Gospel will know that the life of which Christ is speaking here is a spiritual life — a spiritual life which has both a vertical and a horizontal aspect. Vertically, it is a life of constant and intimate fellowship with God, made possible by the mediation of His Son. Horizontally, it is a life of Christian action, sharing the good things of God with all with whom it comes in contact. Of that life, Christ says: "I am come that they might have it and that they might have a surplus of it."

There is a subtle inference (perhaps not so subtle) in the words of Christ, "I have come in order that they might have life." The inference is that without Him there *is* no life — that is, no spiritual life in the sense spoken of in the previous paragraph. It so happens that that inference is more than an inference. It is an explicit presupposition of the Christian Gospel. Christ came to bring spiritual life to a humanity that was spiritually dead and which, apart from Him, is still dead.

Listen to what the apostle Paul wrote to a little group of Christians in Ephesus: "To you who were spiritually *dead* . . . Christ has given *life!* . . . But even though we were dead in our sins, God was so rich in mercy that He gave us the very life of Christ" (Eph. 2:1-5 Phillips). Again and again he refers to believers as (spiritually) dead people who had been brought to life by the good news about Christ. Dead once, but now alive.

Christ Himself said essentially the same thing to Nicodemus, one of the VIPs of his day. "I tell you the truth," He said, "no one can see the kingdom of God unless he is born again" (John 3:3). In other words, the new life which Christ is prepared to give is not merely a matter of reformation (a changing or revamping of the old), it is rather a matter of regeneration: a creation of something new, something that wasn't there before. To quote Paul once more, "When anyone is joined to Christ he is a new being: the old is gone, the new has come." (2 Cor. 5:17)

So it is to (spiritually) dead men today, men whose lives have never been quickened by the saving grace of God through the Gospel, that Christ says: "I have come in order that you might have life and that you might have a surplus of it. First, that you might have life. And then, that you might have a surplus of it."

But how make application for this life? Strange as it may seem, you don't have to make any application! God is applying to you! The Christian Gospel in its very nature is an *announcement,* the announcement that God has redeemed every man, woman, and child of the human race from spiritual death and has won for him a glorious spiritual life. He has accomplished this redemption through the birth, the life, the death and resurrection of His Son.

By His substitutionary death for all mankind, Christ, the eternal Son of God, has won a universal amnesty. He has brought about a complete reconciliation between God and man. In short, everything that was wrong between man and his Maker has been made right by the redeeming, reconciling work of God's own Son. Any man who believes *that* has, indeed, taken a lease on a new life! A new life created and bestowed by God Himself.

The apostle Paul makes this claim in his Letter to the Romans. After writing to them at length about the redeeming work of Christ and reminding them how they had become the children of God through faith in Christ's redemption, he writes these significant words (we quote them at length, since they give us a beautiful blending of Christian *faith* and *life*):

"Since, then, it is by faith that we are justified, let us grasp the fact that we have peace with God through our Lord Jesus Christ. Through Him we have confidently entered into this new relationship of grace; and here we take our stand, in happy certainty of the glorious things He has for us in the future."

He goes on to say: "This doesn't mean, of course, that we have only a hope of *future* joys. We can be full of joy *here and now* even in our trials and troubles. Taken in the right spirit, these very things will give us patient endurance; this in turn will develop a mature character, and a character of this sort produces a steady hope, a hope that will never disappoint us.

"Already we have some experience of the love of God flooding through our hearts by the Holy Spirit given to us. And we can see that it was while we were powerless to help ourselves that Christ died for sinful men. . . . The proof of God's amazing love is this: that it was *while we were sinners* that Christ died for us. Moreover, if He did that for us while we were sinners, now that we are men justified by the shedding of His blood, what reason have we to fear the wrath of God? If, while we were His enemies, Christ reconciled us to God by *dying for us,* surely now that we are reconciled we may be perfectly certain of our salvation through His *living in us.* Nor, I am sure, is this a matter of bare salvation — we may hold our heads high in the light of God's love because of the reconciliation which Christ has made." (Rom. 5:1-11 Phillips)

That is the real philosophy of the Christian life. Indeed, that *is* the Christian life. And of that life Christ says: "I have come that they might have a surplus of it." What are the plusses of the Christian life? Among many others, the Bible lists the following:

Pardon. One day the people brought a young paralytic to Jesus to see if He could heal him. When Jesus perceived how great the faith of the young man was, He greeted him with a familiar greeting which became thematic of His entire ministry: "Courage, My son!" He said. "Your sins are forgiven" (Matt. 9:2). And then He proceeded to cure the young man's paralysis. Forgiveness was the central theme of His ministry, and it continues to be the central theme of the Gospel today.

The very first plus of the Christian faith has always been, and will always continue to be, the great plus of divine pardon, of knowing that the blood of Jesus Christ, God's Son, has erased our entire guilty record. Morning, noon, and night the believer can hear the assuring voice of Christ: "Courage! My son! Your sins are forgiven." They are forgiven because He Himself has paid for them.

Peace. Many books have been written on the subject of peace of mind and peace of soul. The Christian finds his peace of mind in Christ. On the evening before His crucifixion Christ spoke what might be called a farewell address to His discouraged and despondent disciples. One of the choice sentences of that address reads: "Peace I leave with you; *My own* peace I give you. I do not give it to you as the world does. Do not be worried and upset; do not be afraid" (John 14:27). The peace which Christ gives to His believers is utterly unique — it is "His own" peace, not the kind "the world" speaks of.

It is first and foremost peace with God, that peace which was made possible by the vicarious life and death and resurrection of God's own Son. As the apostle Paul put it: "Now that we have been put right with God through faith, we have peace with God through our Lord Jesus Christ" (Rom. 5:1). Christ has made us "right with God"! He has put us back into God's good graces. He has reestablished a Father-son, Father-daughter relationship between God and the believer. Through His divine atonement for human guilt He has brought about a perfect reconciliation (2 Cor. 5:17-19) between God and man. And the result? Man can be at peace — true peace, at peace with God and, therefore, at peace with himself and, as far as the individual believer is concerned, at peace with all men (Rom. 12:18). That is the kind of peace Christ offers.

Near the end of his letter to the Philippians Paul writes: "Don't worry about anything. . . . God's peace, which is far beyond human understanding, will keep your hearts and minds safe, in Christ Jesus" (Phil. 4:6-7). In the original Greek there is a dramatic picture behind that word "keep." It might be translated: "God's peace will stand guard (as an armored soldier) at the entry of your heart and mind, watching, guarding, and protecting." *That* peace is another plus of the Christian faith.

Assurance. The person who has put his hand into the hand of Christ will find an assurance which he can find nowhere else. Frequently Christ compared the relationship between Himself and the believer to that which existed between a shepherd and his sheep on the distant hills of Palestine. The shepherd's attitude was normally that of unfailing solicitude for the welfare of his sheep, and the attitude of the individual sheep was that of unquestioning trust in the shepherd. So Christ's reassuring words to His disciples were fraught with meaning when He said: "I am the Good Shepherd. As the Father knows Me and I know the Father, in the same way I know My sheep and they know Me. And I am willing to die for them. . . . My sheep listen to My voice; I know them, and they follow Me. I give them eternal life, and they shall never

die; and no one can snatch them away from Me."
(John 10:14-15, 27-28)

Read those last two lines once more! Remember
who spoke them! Jesus Christ Himself! His word is
as good as He Himself. He will not go back on it.
His promise is clear: "Put your life into My hands and
you will be forever safe. No one will ever snatch you
from My grasp." The man who truly believes that
can not only start living, he can start living on his
surplus: the fathomless promises of God in Christ.

Joy. Joy is one of the theme words of the Christian Gospel and therefore also of the Christian faith
and life. Already on the night of Christ's birth the
angel announced: "Fear not, for, behold, I bring you
good tidings of great *joy* which shall be to all people,
for unto you is born this day in the city of David a
Savior, which is Christ the Lord" (Luke 2:10 KJV).
That is more than beautiful English. It is sublime truth.
The entry of Christ into the world on that first Christ-
mas night as well as His entry into millions of hearts
and lives ever since has created immeasurable joy.
The New Testament brims with such expressions as
joy, *much* joy, rejoice, and gladness. Christ intended
joy to be one of the hallmarks of the Christian life.
On the night before His death He told His disciples
that He had shared the message of His Gospel with
them "so that My joy may be in you, and that your
joy may be complete." (John 15:11)

There can be no doubt that when Christ said:
"I have come in order that they might have life, and
that they might have a surplus of it," He included this
deep and abiding joy of the Christian heart as one of
the plusses of His Gospel.

Heaven. Heaven is not a popular word today. It has been associated by many with a sort of "pie in the sky" outlook on life. That, however, is a caricature of what Christ actually taught. Anyone who will read the four gospels without prejudice will agree that Christ was very much concerned and very much involved with the nitty-gritty problems of the perplexing here and now; but underlying and overarching all of these problems was the problem of man's eternal destiny, and to that He directed Himself again and again. Not only the concept but also the sure promise of eternal life was frequently on His lips.

Before He raised dead Lazarus from the grave, He comforted Lazarus' sister Martha with the memorable words: "I am the resurrection and the life. Whoever believes in Me will live, even though he dies; and whoever lives and believes in Me will never die" (John 11:25-26). In His great intercessory prayer, in which He included all believers of all times, Christ said to His Father: "This is eternal life: for men to know You, the only true God, and to know Jesus Christ, whom You sent." (John 17:3)

That He was not merely speaking of some vague sort of "immortality" is clear from such intimate and concrete assurances as His well-known words spoken, again, shortly before He would be removed from His beloved disciples by an excruciating death: "Do not be worried and upset," He said. "Believe in God, and believe also in Me. There are many rooms in my Father's house, and I am going to prepare a place for you. I would not tell you this if it were not so. And after I go and prepare a place for you, I will come back and take you to myself, so that *you* will be where

I am" (John 14:1-3). Books could be written on those marvelously reassuring words. Suffice it here to say: Jesus Christ did not hesitate to hold out the sure prospect of heaven as a source of inspiration, courage, and hope to those who believed in Him.

Nor did His disciples after Him. The apostle Paul spoke again and again of the sure hope of the resurrection, basing his assurance not only on the clear and unmistakable promise of Christ but also on the fact that Christ had already delivered on His promise: *He Himself had risen from the grave!* In Christ's resurrection Paul saw the assurance of our resurrection, and so he climaxes the remarkable fifteenth chapter of his first letter to the Corinthians with the well-known song of triumph: "O Death, where is thy sting? O Grave, where is thy victory? . . . Thanks be to God which giveth *us* the victory through our Lord Jesus Christ!" (1 Cor. 15:55-57 KJV). Yes, the Christian Gospel proclaims the sure prospect of a resurrection — and of a heaven.

Pardon! Peace! Assurance! Joy! Eternal life with Jesus Christ in heaven! Those are some of the plusses of the Christian faith and life. Those are some of the *sur-plusses* on which you can begin living today. Those and much more await every man, woman, or child who enters into sonship with the Father through a simple trust in Jesus Christ, His Son.

CHAPTER SIX

You Can Get Rhyme and Reason Out of Your Life

Have you ever found yourself all confused, looking at a road map, unable to make head or tail out of it, and then suddenly noticing that you hadn't unfolded it completely? There was still another flap to be unfolded, and it was on *that* section of the map that many of the tangled and twisted highways finally converged. Once you unfolded the final flap, everything began to make sense.

It's very much the same with life.

Any man who tries to get rhyme and reason out of human existence, while confining his perspective to the few short years between his birth and death, is bound to come up with little rhyme and far less reason. He is working with a map which hasn't been completely unfolded, and too many of the crisscrossed highways seem to end up nowhere. The fact is, human existence doesn't end with death. There's another flap which will have to be unfolded before the pattern is completed.

If ever there was a time when human life seemed to make little sense (we mean that part of it which lies between the signing of our birth certificate and the filing of our death certificate), that time is now.

For every question modern man has answered he has raised another for which he has *no* answer.

He gets born. He grows. He gets sick. He gets well. He acquires a measure of sense through the slow and painful process of education. He eats, he sleeps, he works. He works, he sleeps, he eats. He repeats this process — until, mysteriously, the highway bleeds off the margin of the only map he knows. But why must he continue the daily struggle? Just to wear out and be discarded like an old suit of clothes? Just to move on and make room for others? He's not quite sure.

Meanwhile he does his best not to think about certain questions. But they have a way of intruding themselves into his consciousness — just when he doesn't want to hear of them. Is there a God? If there is, what kind of God is He? How could He let the world get into the mess it's in — with all the pain, the hatred, the suffering, the bloodshed? How could He let His world degenerate into the madhouse it is today? Specifically, what does He think of *me?* What does He intend to do with me? How do I, little I, fit into His plans for the universe, particularly His plans for the human family? What is my personal relationship to Him — and His to me?

If there is a God, why does He permit so much tragedy to crowd into my life? My unemployment, my hospital bills, my bitter disappointments, my failures, my heartaches? Why did little Margie have to die at six, while Grandfather at eighty is lingering with an incurable disease? Is there any intelligent plan that lies behind all this? anything that can give it meaning?

And what about a life beyond the grave? Will there really be a resurrection? If so, what is to become of me, my wife, my children? Will my destiny in any life beyond the grave be determined by what I do today? Tomorrow? Am I at this moment forging the shackles which will imprison my soul and body in all eternity? Is there really a hell? If so, how can I escape it? Is there really a heaven? If so, how can I be assured that I am going there?

Whether a man lives in Chicago, Cleveland, or New York, in Bombay, Calcutta, or Shanghai, these questions have a way of insinuating themselves into his thinking — sometimes whispering, sometimes shouting, but always crying for an answer. And unless he has an authoritative road map of human existence which is *fully opened* — including the flap on which all the devious highways of his life are destined to converge — he will be unable to come up with a satisfactory answer.

God has given you the answer — in the pages of your Bible. At least, enough of the answer to let you know that there *is* a pattern and that the pattern is in His hand. God wants you to view your life not by a perspective which is limited by human birth on the one end and human death on the other, but by a perspective which on the left has you and God in eternity past and on the right has you and God in eternity future. (Strictly speaking, there can be no "eternity past" or "eternity future." Time and eternity do not mesh. These terms are an accommodation to the limitations of the human mind.)

The fact is that God had you in His mind already in eternity past, and He wants to have you at His side in eternity future. Birth and death are mere incidents in God's completed plan for you. Until you unfold those two flaps — the one on the left, before your birth, and the one on the right, after your death — you are not going to get much rhyme and reason out of the tangled lines that lie between.

Before the world began, God determined to send His Son into the world to redeem you so that you could live with Him after the world itself had ended. You were the object of His concern long before He put the sun, the moon, and the stars in their places. And He wants to keep you the object of His concern long after the sun, the moon, and the stars will be gone forever.

The Bible tells us that God has created us for eternal fellowship with Him. It says: "He saved us and called us to be His own people, not because of what we have done, but because of His own purpose and grace. He gave this grace to us in Christ Jesus *before the beginning of time,* but now it has been revealed to us through the appearing of our Savior, Jesus Christ. For Christ has ended the power of death, and through the Good News (the Gospel) He has revealed immortal life" (2 Tim. 1:9-10). Note the phrase which we have italicized in the above passage. In another place the Bible speaks of "everlasting life which God, who cannot lie, promised *before the beginning of time."* (Titus 1:2 Phillips)

That is the first point you'll have to pin down if you ever want to get rhyme and reason out of human life, particularly out of *your* life. God thought of you before He rolled the sun into its present course. Before He studded the summer sky with myriads of stars, He plotted a course by which He could bring you into eternal fellowship with Him. He decided to save you for time and for eternity through the miracle of the cross, the sacrificial death of His own beloved Son.

And the second point is this. The plan which God has charted for your life is not going to end in a cemetery. Just as that plan had its origin in an eternity which lies behind us, so it will have its complete fulfillment in an eternity which lies before us. We'll never *begin* to understand His ways with us until we realize there's a flap of the map which has not yet been unfolded, and we'll never *fully* understand His ways until He Himself unfolds that final page.

Presumptuous as it may sound, it is a fact nevertheless that only the man who has seen in Jesus Christ the Son of God and Savior of his soul can ever hope to get rhyme and reason out of living. Only the man who can see God loving him in eternity past, who can see Christ redeeming him in eternity present, and who can see God welcoming him into blissful fellowship with Him throughout eternity future, can fit the jigsaw pieces of his life into a pattern that is meaningful and purposeful.

That, in fact, is the Christian Gospel. "Whatever we may have to go through now," the Bible says, "is less than nothing compared with the magnificent future God has planned for us. The whole creation is on tiptoe to see the wonderful sight of the sons of God coming into their own. . . . It is plain to anyone with eyes to see that at the present time all created life groans in a sort of universal travail. And it is plain, too, that we who have a foretaste of the Spirit are in a state of painful tension, while we wait for that re-demption of our bodies, which will mean that at last we have realized our full sonship in Him." (Rom. 8:18-23 Phillips)

Now, what does all this mean in terms of the ordinary washday for the lady of the house or in terms of the daily grind at the workbench or at the office? Everything! It means that if a person has put his eternal destiny into the hands of God through faith in Jesus Christ, he knows that no matter how tangled the skein of his life may seem, the threads are in the hands of a loving Father; and in the hands of a loving Father they are bound to have a loving purpose in the pattern He has planned. It was this assurance that prompted the well-known lines:

My life is but a weaving
    Between my Lord and me,
I cannot choose the colors
    He worketh steadily.
Ofttimes He weaveth sorrow,
    And I in foolish pride
Forget He sees the "upper"
    And I the "under" side.

Not till the loom is silent
    And the shuttles cease to fly,
Shall God unroll the canvass
    And explain the reason why
The dark threads are as needful
    In the weaver's skillful hand
As the threads of gold and silver
    In the pattern He has planned.

The Bible puts it this way: "To those who love God, who are called according to His plan, everything that happens fits into a *pattern for good*" (Rom. 8:28 Phillips). Only after we have been convinced that God really loves us, that because of the redeeming life and death and resurrection of His Son He has accepted us as children in His family, and that since we are His children, we are also His heirs (heirs of eternal life with Christ in heaven) — only after we have been convinced of these things, can we really be sure that everything that happens to us "fits into a *pattern for good.*"

In short, only the believer in Christ can, in the ultimate sense, get rhyme and reason out of living. For a complete explanation of some of the painful sideroads and twisted byways of his life he may have to wait until the final flap of the map has been unfolded — the flap which brings him finally to the city of his God. But, at least, he knows there is still another page, and he knows that God Himself has promised that when the final page has been unfolded, it will vindicate His wisdom and His *love*.

CHAPTER SEVEN

You Can Be
"Good for Something"

In the fine arts building at the Seattle World's Fair there was an oddity which captured the attention and held the interest of thousands of people every day.

Called the Monomatic, it was a huge contraption with many moving parts—old bicycle wheels, roller skates, kitchen utensils, parts of old automobiles, sleds, radiators, hub caps, and discarded gears of all descriptions.

At regular intervals a motor would start and the whole contraption would go into hilarious action—wheels spinning, pistons pumping, whistles tooting, metal clanking, and bells ringing.

And what was it for? What was it supposed to accomplish? Nothing! It was not *designed* to accomplish anything. Its purpose was merely to get its various parts into awkward motion for the amusement of the public. That was all its original creator had in mind.

Like the Monomatic, many people, including some who profess to be followers of Christ, spend their whole lives merely "going through the motions." There is a sense in which they can be called good, but there is also a sense in which they can be called good *for nothing.* They are in reality Monomatics, spinning their wheels impressively, and yet of no earthly good to their neighbor or to the society in which they live. Their attitude and behavior are really caricatures of the genuine Christian faith and life.

There is a significant passage in Paul's letter to the Ephesians which is very pertinent here. After impressing on his readers that they have been saved from their corrupt ways only by the grace of God, through Christ, he immediately goes on to say "we are His workmanship, created in Christ Jesus *for good works,* which God prepared beforehand, that we should walk in them" (Eph. 2:10 RSV) "Good works" is the Biblical term for "good deeds." Different translators have rendered this remarkable passage in different ways. Some say that, according to this passage, the Christian has been "cut out for good deeds." Others claim that Paul wanted to emphasize that each believer in Christ "has his work cut out for him."

In either case the essential meaning is the same. The person who puts his trust in Christ as Savior and Lord has not only been re-created; he has been custom built for a specific purpose: for doing good. "Created in Christ Jesus *for good works.*" He has been designed, equipped, and tooled to serve his fellowman, and through such service to serve his God. That is the relationship which the Bible establishes between Christian faith and action. We have been redeemed by Christ for time and for eternity. That is our faith. That is our Spirit-given assurance. But we have been redeemed for a purpose. And an important part of that purpose is Christian action — Christian deeds that flow from Christian faith. When writing to his Corinthian converts, Paul put this truth in another way. "God bought you for a price," he wrote. "So use your bodies for God's glory" (1 Cor. 6:20). The redeemed of God are to be His effective agents, carrying out His will, and serving His world.

Our purpose here is not to write a tract on Christian activism. That would go beyond the scope and purpose of this book. Our intention is rather to encourage the believer in Christ to live up to the purpose for which he is *designed* and thus to achieve his God-intended sense of fulfillment. To live above our circumstances, we will have to live for others. That is not only good psychology, it is good theology. And it is good Christianity. Down through the years this writer has received hundreds of letters from miserable Christians (perhaps we should rather say, Christians who were miserable) who lamented their general unhappiness. Why, despite their sincere profession of faith in Christ as Lord and Savior, were their minds so constantly preoccupied with thoughts of gloom and doom, they wanted to know. In many cases it was quite evident that the writers of such letters were living lives that were completely turned in on themselves. The doors and windows of their minds had all been locked, and they had been locked from the inside. And so, day after day, all they had to live with were their personal aches and pains, their personal fears, frustrations, and forebodings.

What they needed was to throw the doors and windows of their lives open, to get *out* — yes, to get out of their own lives and into the lives of others. They needed to remember that they are "God's workmanship, created in Christ Jesus for good works." In the carrying out of that purpose they will find fulfillment, and in that sense of fulfillment they will find an ever growing sense of satisfaction. It may sound like a strange contradiction, but living above our circumstances will sometimes mean living below the burdens of others. Jesus said something similar when He told His followers that whoever would lose his life for Christ's sake would find it (Matt. 10:39). Many a person has lost himself in the service of others, and in doing so has found the inner glow of personal fulfillment he so desperately needed.

Surely, in a world such as ours today there is no lack of opportunity for the believer in Christ to be "good — for something." With two thirds of the world's population going to bed hungry every night, with poverty a way of life for hundreds of millions, with racial strife and bitterness simmering close to the boiling point, with the moral standards of our Western world sinking ever more deeply into a bottomless morass, there is no dearth of opportunity for the believer in Christ to be active in translating his *vertical* faith into *horizontal* action.

There is no joy in the heart of a plaster saint. But there *can* be joy, much joy, in the heart of the believer in Christ whose day-to-day life is devoted to selfless service to his fellowman.

CHAPTER EIGHT

You've Got Something to Celebrate

The elevator boy gave the white-haired man a cheery smile as he stepped into the elevator. It was early in the morning, and the elderly gentleman was his very first passenger.

Up and up the elevator soared, and as it did, the boy continued to whistle a merry tune. "Why so happy?" the dignified man inquired. Stopping his whistling just long enough to form his words, the bright-eyed boy replied: "I've never lived this day before!"

What a thought! If only all of us could grasp it — and live it! If only each of us could greet the dawn of each new day with the same wisdom, the same exuberance, the same spirit of adventure. The thought, of course, was not original with the young man in the elevator. Some three thousand years ago King David, whom the Bible calls "a man after God's own heart," wrote in one of his psalms: "What a wonderful day the Lord has given us; let us be happy, let us celebrate!" (Ps. 118:24). Those who are more familiar with the King James Version of the Scriptures will remember the above passage as "This is the day which the Lord hath made; we will rejoice and be glad in it."

But can we actually say that — and mean it? Is *today,* the day on which you are reading this page, actually a day that God has made — and a day in which we are to be happy and celebrate? For the believer in Christ the answer to those questions is an unequivocal yes. This *is* a day that has come to us from the hand of God, a day we have never lived before, a day in which we are to rejoice and be glad and to celebrate.

Now, all of this of course would be just so much soupy sentimentality were it not solidly anchored in a firm foundation of Biblical truth. The apostle Paul wrote to the Christians at Rome: "Now that we have been put right with God through faith, we have peace with God through our Lord Jesus Christ. He has brought us, by faith, into *the grace of God in which we now stand.* We rejoice, then, in the hope we have of sharing God's glory!" (Rom. 5:1). And then he proceeds to enumerate the reasons a believer in Christ has for rejoicing. But the words we wish to underscore in the above passage are those which we have italicized, namely "the grace of God in which we now stand."

You and I can celebrate today, not because we received an unexpected check in the mail, not because the boss gave us a promotion, not because we are enjoying radiant health, but, above all, because it is another day of *grace.* As a result of what Christ has done for us, you and I are living in a day-to-day relationship with God which is utterly unique. The Bible calls it a relationship of grace — grace meaning, in this instance, the unmerited mercy of God revealed through Jesus Christ. You and I are living every moment of our lives "in God's love."

There are some very religious people who completely misunderstand this relationship and as a result make themselves most miserable. While they might deny it they, in effect, picture God as a cruel tyrant who is keeping His eye on them, waiting for them to make the first false move, ready to mete out sudden punishment. To them, if we may exaggerate a little to make our point, God is a mean and humorless bookkeeper who is engaged in an endless balancing of the ledger, entering minute-by-minute debits and credits opposite their names—for instance, sixty-seven sins committed on Thursday, sixty-six repented of on Friday, leaving a balance of one still unrepented and unforgiven.

In other words, they picture their slate as being alternately clean and alternately filled with accusing entries, depending upon when they last sinned and when they last asked God's forgiveness. That is a caricature of the Christian faith! For the believer in Christ, the slate is *always* clean. No accusing debits mar its face. That is the tremendous revelation of the Christian Gospel. We are not the clients of a heavenly bookkeeper. We are the children of a heavenly Father—His *forgiven* children. Through faith in Christ we have stepped *out* of that tit-for-tat relationship with God into which we were born by nature, and by which we could expect nothing else from God but our just deserts; and we have stepped into a new relationship in which we can expect nothing but His love, His mercy and compassion. Or to put this almost incredible revelation into the language of the Scriptures, we have stepped out of the relationship of Law into the relationship of grace. And in *this* relationship, we can be sure, we start each and every day with a clean slate. Christ has seen to that.

What a difference this should make for the believer in Christ as he goes about the daily business of living. He has it on God's authority that he can hang loose, that he can relax, that he has a Father in heaven who not only knows him but loves him. Loves him so much that He gave him His Son. Some time ago we heard a father soothing his five-year-old daughter who had come running into the house crying because of some minor hurt. After wiping away her tears, he put his arm around her and said simply: "Cheer up! God loves you." We know, of course, that, spoken in some families, such comfort could be empty and meaningless. But not in that family! Here was a family that was living every day consciously and joyously in God's grace. Christ had given every member of that family a clean slate, and with that slate had come not only the full assurance of God's grace but also the fruits which are bound to follow: peace, hope, love, and joy. It meant very much to that little girl to be reminded of the pivotal fact of her life—"God loves you."

Christianity is, in a very real sense, a call to celebrate, to rejoice daily in the revelation of God's love. St. Peter wrote to the early Christians who had just come to faith in Christ: "You love Him, although you have not seen Him; you believe in Him, although you do not now see Him; and so you rejoice with *a great and glorious joy,* which words cannot express, because you are obtaining the purpose of your faith, the salvation of your souls" (1 Peter 1:8-9). Ever since they had heard the "good news" of Christ, theirs had been a life of continuous spiritual celebration.

Similarly, the apostle Paul proclaimed a Gospel of spiritual joy. To the believers at Philippi he wrote: "Delight yourselves in God . . . find your joy in Him . . . . Don't worry over anything whatever . . . and the peace of God, which transcends human understanding, will keep constant guard over your hearts and minds as they rest in Christ Jesus" (Phil. 4:4 Phillips). If these exhortations to celebration, to joy and carefreeness, seem exaggerated to the casual reader, let him remember that the New Testament call to celebrate is addressed only to those who are carrying in their hearts the clean slates referred to earlier in this chapter—only to those who, by faith in Christ, have stepped into the glorious relationship of grace. By God's grace, through Christ, they have no marks against them. And they have an omnipotent Savior at their side. And so they rejoice continually.

The early Christians gathered regularly to celebrate their new relationship to God. They celebrated in private and in public. And so have Christians in all ages. Today millions celebrate the love of God in Christ from moment to moment, from day to day. The young mother tending her newborn child; the young father at his desk, his workbench, or in the assembly line; the laborer shivering with the rat-a-tat-tat of his electric drill; the teacher in her classroom; the patient on her hospital bed; the elderly man in the nursing home—all can celebrate, in their hearts and lives, the unspeakable love of God.

One of the highest purposes of public worship is public celebration. Those who have entered into a relationship with God, based solely on His abounding grace, gather in their sanctuaries to shout their praises: to sing hymns and anthems of joy. Joy for a thousand reasons but, above all, for the fact that through Christ their slates have been washed clean: their guilt has been erased: their sins have been forgiven, and God is "on their side." (Rom. 8:31)

It was a man who knew beyond the shadow of a doubt that he was living in God's grace who wrote almost three thousand years ago: "What a wonderful day the Lord has given us: let us be happy, let us celebrate!" (Ps. 118:24)

Can you say that? You can—through Christ, the Savior.

CHAPTER NINE

You'd Better Believe It!

We are living in a day of sensational offers. National advertisers seem to be vying with one another to make the most preposterous claims and the most unbelievable offers. "If you don't have that soft, smooth, velvety complexion after using Miracle Soap only one week, just return the wrapper, and we'll be happy to refund your money." Or "if you don't feel like a new man after taking only one bottle of Wonder Tonic, your dealer will refund twice the cost of the bottle." Who hasn't heard these or similar claims and offers?

Anyone who has listened to the ridiculous claims being made over radio and television for an almost endless parade of products by various sponsors will surely have come to the conclusion that the advertisers themselves don't expect the public to believe them. Almost any claim will do—as long as it provides an opportunity to repeat the brand name at least a half a dozen times.

Americans have taken these extravagant claims in gradually increasing doses until they are almost completely inoculated against them. From here on no offer—no matter how "stupendous" or "colossal"—will ever be taken seriously. And the simple reason is: Americans have been sensationalized into a state of mind which is beyond sensation.

The tragedy of it all is that the one really fantastic announcement, which every man, woman, and child on the face of the globe should hear, has been drowned in the din and confusion of these exaggerated claims. And when this one really stupendous announcement occasionally does get through to the ear of an individual, he is inclined to regard it as just another preposterous claim—just another unbelievable offer.

The fact is, there is *one miraculous claim* which happens to be gloriously and eternally true and which lies at the basis of every promise in these pages. If you want to be able to live above your circumstances, if you want to have access to the only source of true spiritual power, if you want to be able to live with yourself and to enjoy your own company, if you want to find something to live for, if you want to get rhyme and reason out of your life, if you want to start living on your surplus, if you really want to celebrate life in the manner which God intended, and, above all, if you want to be able to face death calm and unafraid, assured of a happy eternity beyond the grave, there is one fantastic claim you must confront and which, pray God, you will believe. And this is it:

Jesus Christ, the eternal Son of God, came down from heaven to earth to pay the penalty of your transgressions, to ransom your life for time and for eternity, and to secure for you a place in the mansions of His Father's house above. That is, indeed, a fantastic claim! But that, and nothing less, is the Christian Gospel! Only he who accepts that claim in faith can experience the sensational satisfaction which it offers.

The Christian Gospel, let it be clearly understood,

is, above all else, a message of redemption—redemption from the guilt, the power, and the punishment of sin. The Bible has very much to say about that ugly little word "sin" and the disastrous havoc it has wrought upon the human race. In order to come to terms with life in the Christian sense, we must come to terms (God's terms) with that devastating little three-letter word.

The Scripture makes it very clear that sin is both a *condition* and an *act*. It is the former before it becomes the latter. When speaking of sin as a condition, the Bible uses such expressions as being born in sin, as being under the dominion of sin, as being not only separated from God but also alienated from Him. It speaks in these dark and tragic terms of man as he is by nature. Not only of *some* men but of the entire human family. For instance, the apostle Paul writes to the Galatians: "But Scripture has declared the whole world to be prisoners in subjection to sin, so that faith in Jesus Christ may be the ground on which the promised blessing is given" (Gal. 3:22). The "whole world" is in subjection to sin, he says, enthralled by its power. There are no exceptions.

The Bible also uses the word sin with reference to those individual thoughts and words and deeds which grow out of man's fractured relationship with God. Greed, lust, envy, pride, selfishness, hatred, murder, sexual impurity—these and many more the Bible labels as transgressions of the law of God and clearly calls them sins. They are sins which widen the gulf which already exists between man and God, as the Old Testament prophets repeatedly pointed out (Is. 59:2). They are sins which invite the wrath of

God upon the individual and on society. Let there be no blinking the fact: sin *is* serious in God's sight. As Paul puts it, "The wages of sin is death" – physical, spiritual, and eternal. (Rom. 6:23 KJV)

While registering at a hotel in San Francisco some time ago, we were struck by the levity with which the world regards the entire concept of sin. On the registration desk lay a small attractive folder with the title "Where to Sin in San Francisco." A hasty scanning of its pages revealed that, in the main, it advertised the better dining places of the city. To the advertising agency responsible for the folder, "sin" evidently was more or less synonymous with enjoying oneself – and nothing more.

That is a treacherous caricature of the Bible's concept of sin. The fact is that until you have been struck down and terrified by the utter *seriousness* of sin, you will have little taste for the Christian Gospel. But once you have come to a piercing awareness of your personal guilt in the sight of God and of your personal inability to do anything about it, you will begin to understand and appreciate the miraculous claim of the inspired Scripture: the announcement that Jesus Christ, the eternal Son of God, came down from heaven to pay the penalty of your transgression, and to redeem your life for time and for eternity.

That is what the Bible means when it speaks of the *redemption* of the human race by the life, the death, and the resurrection of Jesus Christ, the Son of God. Christ has redeemed every human life. Literally, He has "bought it back." He has bought it back from the power of sin and death. Miraculous and incredible as that may seem, that is the heart of the Christian Gospel! Fantastic!

Listen to these clear statements of the Bible: "There is no difference at all: all men have sinned and are far away from God's saving presence. But by the free gift of God's grace they are all put right with Him through Christ Jesus, who sets them free. God offered Him so that by His death He should become the means by which men's sins are forgiven, through their faith in Him" (Rom. 3:22-25). St. Peter tells us: "You know what was paid to set you free . . . . It was not something . . . such as silver or gold; you were set free by the costly sacrifice of Christ, who was like a lamb without defect or spot" (1 Peter 1:18 to 19). St. Paul told the early Christians: "You do not belong to yourselves but to God; He bought you for a price" (1 Cor. 6:19). Christ Himself said that He had come into the world to "give His life to redeem many people" (Matt. 28:20). In the language of the Bible we have been purchased, bought, redeemed, ransomed! Christ paid the ransom when He died on the cross for the sins of all mankind.

Perhaps most marvelous of all the statements of the Bible concerning Christ's death (as God's own payment for human guilt) are these words of the prophet Isaiah, written about seven hundred years before Christ was born: "Surely, *He* hath borne *our* griefs and carried *our* sorrows . . . . *He* was wounded for *our* transgressions, *He* was bruised for *our* iniquities. The chastisement of *our* peace was upon *Him*, and with *His* stripes *we* are healed. All we like sheep have gone astray; we have turned everyone to his own way; and the Lord hath laid on *Him* the iniquity of *us* all." (Is. 53:4-6 KJV)

The Bible leaves no doubt concerning the redeeming purpose and the redeeming power of Christ's death. As the eternal Son of God, He died as all men's Substitute. And He arose again on Easter morning to show all men everywhere that the ransom was complete, that the Father in heaven had accepted the payment of His Son for the redemption of all mankind (Rom. 4:25). The resurrection of Christ is God's own signature to every miraculous claim of the Christian Gospel. It is God's "yes" to the Christian Gospel. It is God's own affirmation of everything Christ ever said or did or promised.

Now what does all of this mean in terms of *your* life — as it is lived 2,000 years after the payment of the ransom? It means that every sin you've ever committed, every wrong you've ever done, was placed upon the shoulders of God's Son. It means that because of His death — in your place — you have been acquitted. Because of His death in your place you can stand today in the presence of your Maker — justified, cleared, forgiven.

But it means more. It means that because of this acquittal your *entire* relationship to God has been completely and forever changed — not only in some distant life to come, but also right here, right now. Because of Christ's great work of reconciliation, the Creator of the universe has become your loving *Father*. Through Christ you have been restored to sonship. (Gal. 3:26; 4:4-7)

And it is by virtue of this happy sonship — this relationship of a trusting child to a loving father — that you have access to the only source of true spiritual power, that you can begin living above your circumstances, that you can find something to live for, and that you can begin to get rhyme and reason out of your everyday existence. Above all, it is by virtue of this happy sonship with the Father that you can look forward to your journey's end calm and unafraid, knowing that through Christ you have a loving Father awaiting you on the far side of the valley, waiting to take you home.

Fantastic?

Yes, fantastic! But a fact nevertheless, because we have God's own word for it, spoken again and again throughout the Scripture. Perhaps the simplest, clearest, and most beautiful statement of this Biblical claim and promise are the words of Christ Himself when He said:

"For God so loved the world that He gave His only begotten Son, that whosoever believeth in Him should not perish, but have everlasting life." (John 3:16 KJV)

You'd better believe it!

CHAPTER TEN

The Proof of the Pudding

There are some things in life that can be demonstrated or "proved" on a blackboard. The teacher in the first grade can prove to her children, for instance, that two plus two are four by drawing two apples on the blackboard, then drawing two more apples, and then counting them—one, two, three, four. The high school teacher can demonstrate conclusively on the blackboard why $(a+b)^2$ must always equal $a^2+2ab+b^2$. And the college instructor can demonstrate to his class, beyond the shadow of a doubt, that two parts of hydrogen and one part of oxygen will always give you water.

But there are some things in life that cannot be proved with chalk. Where is there a formula, for instance, that can prove to the weeping child that his mother loves him? Where is the equation that can forever remove the doubts of a disillusioned and distracted wife and convince her of the affection and fidelity of a husband whose faithfulness she has come to question? Who can prove by a plus sign or a minus, by an equation or a test tube, by an airtight syllogism, or by a mile-long series of "Q.E.D.'s," that there is love in the heart of a mother, that there is fidelity in the heart of a husband, that there is beauty in a summer sky, that there is peace in a tranquil landscape, or that there is joy and inspiration in the song of a bird? These things cannot be proved in classrooms or in laboratories — they can be experienced only in the logic and the language of the heart.

It's very much the same with the Christian Gospel. If you are looking for a mathematical formula which will prove all the claims of the Christian faith to be true — before you yourself have tried and tested them — you are doomed to bitter disappointment. That doesn't mean that there isn't much about the Bible that can be proved, even to the unenlightened intellect. Even the unconverted mind, if it is honest, will be impressed by the precise fulfillment of Old Testament prophecies in the life and death and resurrection of Christ, or by the findings of archaeology which again and again have established the historical record of the Bible to be objective truth, or by the undeniable influence for good which the Bible has exerted wherever it has been read and believed and followed, or by the towering strength of the Christian church even in a day like ours when old truths and old values are being challenged and old institutions are being dismantled and discarded. Some of these considerations *do* make a certain impression even on the unconverted intellect. But, in the strictest sense, they do not constitute a *proof* that the religion of Christ is the religion of God.

It lies in the very nature of the Christian message that the only way of "proving" it is *trying* it. A man who is trapped in the fifth story of a burning building and who has been told by firemen to leap into the outstretched net below can do one of two things: He can jump, or he can stand in the window and ask a lot of questions. Will the net really hold him? Are the ropes really stout enough? And how about the men who are spreading the net? Is their grip firm and strong? As long as he stands in the window and insists on answers to all of his questions, he will never know how strong the net is, and if he stands there too long, the probability is that he will perish. If he is to be saved, he will have to *leap* — even *before* every question has been answered. And even if all his questions have been answered, his leap will still have to be an act of faith, because he can never know for sure that the net is as strong as the firemen say it is until he himself has tried it.

In a sense, the Christian faith is a *leap* — not a leap into the dark, but a leap into the promises of God. Christ told the unbelievers of His day: "Whoever is willing to do what God wants will know whether what I teach comes from God or whether I speak on my own authority" (John 7:17). Not argumentation, not a fancy Q.E.D. at the end of a brilliant formula, but a humble "doing of what God wants" is the only way of arriving at spiritual certainty.

And Christ left no doubt as to what it was that God wanted from those to whom He spoke. Christ's primary call to the people of His day (and of our day) can be summed up in two short words: repentance and faith. Again and again we hear Him saying: "Repent! And believe the good news!"

Repent! That is, acknowledge and lament your sinfulness in the sight of God! And believe the "good news"! That is, believe that in Christ you have a divine Savior who has restored you to sonship with the Father. Once you have gone through this experience — of repenting and believing — Christ says, you will know whether His teachings come from God or whether they are of purely human origin.

In other words, the proof of the pudding is in the eating thereof. It's not the picture on the box, it's not even the sight of the pudding itself, but it's the eating of the pudding that tells whether it's good or not. King David, the great sinner and the great saint, had tested the promises of God. And he was thrilled with what he found. "I sought the Lord," he says, and He heard me and delivered me from all my fears! . . . Oh, *taste* and see that the Lord is good! Blessed is the man that trusteth in Him." (Ps. 34: 4, 8 KJV)

Millions of people have tasted — and have found that the Lord is good. They have found that the "good news" of Christ is the power of God. In that Gospel they have found pardon for their sins, peace for their conscience, and power to lead victorious, Christian lives. Nor need we go back to the first Christian century to find lives which have been redeemed and transformed by the power of the Gospel. We need only look about us. We can find compelling testimonials to the power of Christ in uncounted flesh-and-blood demonstrations — not a thousand years or a thousand miles away, but right here and now, perhaps in your own neighborhood, perhaps on your own street, perhaps in your own family.

Every truly dedicated Christian living today is a *witness* of the power of the Gospel! And as a witness, he brings proof of the things which he has seen and heard, of the things which he has tasted, tested, and trusted. Recently we received a note from a clergyman in Baltimore to which he attached a letter written by one of his members, Bill Morgan, a 34-year-old auto-parts salesman. A GI friend up front in an Asian battle area had written to Bill, telling him of his inner conflicts and spiritual uncertainty. From Bill's reply we quote only a few significant paragraphs. Listen to what the good news of the Christian Gospel has done for this auto-parts salesman:

". . . As you know, my church teaches and preaches Christ and Him alone as the only Savior of mankind. As the Bible says, there is no other.

"We are on this earth for only one reason, and that is to worship and glorify God, the Father, the Son, and the Holy Spirit. Well, Gene, that has been my aim, even though I must admit that I have achieved it only in a small way. . . .

"At no time do I worry about anything, because I know that Jesus, my Savior, is always near. One little prayer to Him can bring a host of angels to your side.

"When I go inside my church, I get an inner peace in my heart, and I feel at peace with everyone. It seems as though the troubles and cares I had just vanish. When I hear the sermon, all is peace, because I am assured once more that Christ has died for me.

"Gene, I just can't tell you how I feel. What I have written can't begin to tell you what it means to have Jesus in your heart. There is a satisfaction that words can't describe."

An auto-parts salesman in modern Baltimore and a king in ancient Palestine have witnessed the very same thing! "I sought the Lord, and He heard me, and delivered me from all my fears! . . . Oh, taste and see that the Lord is good! Blessed is the man that trusteth in Him." (Ps. 34:4, 8 KJV)

Dr. Theodore Hanser, M. D., prominent Saint Louis surgeon, recently made this eloquent statement of his faith: "Peace of mind, of conscience, of heart —these are the elusive goals which modern man is seeking like the proverbial pot of gold at the end of the rainbow. But peace of mind can never be found in our accumulation of stocks and bonds and insurance policies. Neither can enduring peace be found in the office of the psychoanalyst. Where then?

"Only in Jesus Christ, the Son of God and Savior of the world, who gave His life that we might live. God knows that I have sinned, and I know it too! But in His mercy He has led me to the Calvary of Good Friday and to the empty tomb of Easter. There I have been assured of my forgiveness. With my hand in His, 'I can do all things through Christ, which strengtheneth me.'"

Lawrence W. Meinzen, lieutenant colonel, U. S. Army, retired, asked very pertinently some time ago: "Have you ever 'spent an eternity' in the few moments that it takes a careening automobile to come to a stop following a head-on collision? *I have!* Or have you ever received the fateful telegram from the Department of Defense stating cryptically: 'The Secretary of Defense regrets to inform you of the death of your son'? *I have!* Or have you ever stood speechless beside the bed of a loved one when the doctor said: 'There is no hope'? *I have!*

"I have experienced personally, or I have witnessed at close range, some of the most piercing pains of life. And I should like to take this opportunity to assure everyone within range of my voice that there is a power capable of overcoming even the severest blows of misfortune. We can avail ourselves of this power through a trusting faith in Jesus Christ, the God-man, who by His own sacrifice on the cross restored us to sonship with the Father. As His child, I need fear no evil."

Louis P. Lochner, Litt. D., Pulitzer Prize winner for Distinguished Foreign Correspondence, in discussing the ethical requirements of a foreign correspondent, expressed his faith in the "good news" of the Christian Gospel in these words: "By the grace of God I have my chart and compass in the Gospel of Christ. Knowing that Jesus is 'the Light of the world,' I know for certain that by following this divine Light I shall not walk in darkness, but shall have the light of life. As I struggle along in my imperfect way to do justice to my exacting calling as an international news analyst, it is comforting to turn to the Scriptures for enlightenment, knowing that 'Thy Word is a lamp unto my feet and a light unto my path.'"

John W. Boehne Jr., former United States Congressman from Indiana, speaking for the record, recently said: "My faith in Jesus Christ as my personal Savior from sin has proved the greatest blessing of my life. His Word has helped me overcome what seemed to be insurmountable circumstances. His Word has comforted me in times of serious illness. His Word has thwarted temptation when temptation seemed so sweet and alluring. In days of doubt and disillusionment His Word has kept me on an even keel. And I know that His Word will be my strength and comfort in the inevitable hour of death."

Every witness quoted in these pages is an active member of a Christian church. Someone may ask: why mention that? In reply we say: to demonstrate that beneath the joy, the peace, and inner satisfaction that each of them has found there lies *a common faith.* Each of them has shared a common creed. Each of them has tasted and tested the same thing, and each has found that "the Lord is good"!

At the fountainhead of their peace and joy there is the same eternal spring. Perhaps no one will ever describe this unfailing source of strength and confident assurance in clearer language than did Martin Luther some four hundred years ago. In his explanation of the Second Article of the Apostles' Creed he spoke the faith of every Christian in these immortal words:

"I believe that Jesus Christ, true God, begotten of the Father from eternity, and also true man, born of the Virgin Mary, is my Lord, who has redeemed me, a lost and condemned creature, purchased and won me from all sins, from death, and from the power of the devil, not with gold or silver, but with His holy, precious blood and with His innocent suffering and death, that I may be His own, and live under Him in His kingdom, and serve Him in everlasting righteousness, innocence, and blessedness, even as He is risen from the dead, lives and reigns to all eternity. This is most certainly true."

The man who stakes his hope for time and for eternity on *that* immovable assurance and lives in day-to-day awareness of all the blessings which it brings can, indeed, stand tall among his fellows. He can live above every circumstance of life.